Contents

Some words are in bold, **like this**. You can find them in the glossary on page 23.

What is a lemur?

A lemur is a **mammal**.

Many mammals have hairy bodies and feed their babies milk.

indri

There are many different types of lemurs.

The biggest lemur is the indri.

What do lemurs look like?

tail

Lemurs have long arms and legs, and often have long tails.

Their strong hands and fingers help them to climb trees.

Lemurs have thick fur that can be brown, black, white, or red.

This lemur has **tufts** of fur around its neck.

Where do lemurs live?

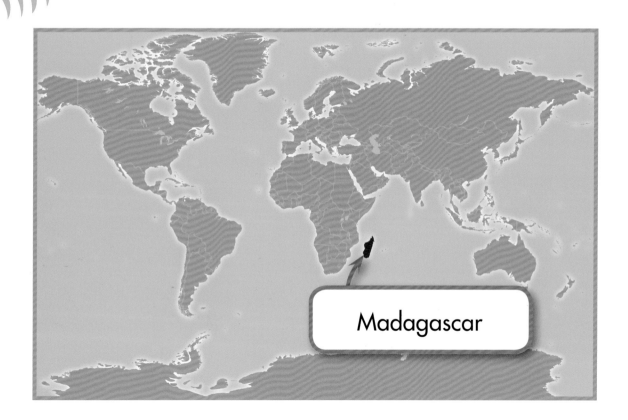

Madagascar

Lemurs live on the island of Madagascar in the Indian Ocean.

Wild lemurs are not found anywhere else on Earth.

The lemurs in this book live in
rainforests on Madagascar.

It is warm and wet in the rainforest
all the year round.

What do lemurs do in the day?

Many types of lemurs wake up when the sun rises.

Then they spend the morning moving through the trees and looking for food.

In the afternoon, some lemurs like to have a rest and sunbathe.

They sit on a branch and stretch their arms out wide.

What do lemurs eat?

Lemurs eat fruit, leaves, and seeds.

They also use their long tongues to reach deep inside flowers for food.

Some lemurs hang upside down from trees to feed.

They hang on to the branches with their feet.

Do lemurs live in groups?

Many lemurs live in groups of up to 20 animals.

A group is called a **troop**.

fossa

Living in a group helps to keep the lemurs safe.

Animals, such as **fossa**, find it easier to attack one lemur than a whole group.

What do lemurs sound like?

Lemurs make lots of different sounds.

They can wail, scream, snort, yap, and groan.

These sounds help the lemurs to keep in touch with each other.

They also warn other groups of lemurs to stay in their own space.

Where are baby lemurs born?

Some baby lemurs are born in nests in the treetops.

The female builds the nest out of twigs, leaves, and moss.

baby

In the day, female lemurs carry their babies with them as they look for food.

Baby lemurs cling to their mother's belly or back.

What do lemurs do at night?

In the evening, the lemurs look for more food to eat.

Then they go to sleep on a branch, or in a hollow tree.

Some rainforest lemurs look for food at night.

Other lemurs move about from time to time during the day and night.

Lemur body map

fur

ear

eye

leg

muzzle

ruff

tail

Glossary

 **fossa** meat-eating animal from Madagascar

 **mammal** animal that feeds its babies milk. Most mammals have hair or fur.

 **rainforest** thick forest with very tall trees and a lot of rain

 **troop** group of lemurs

 **tuft** bunch of something such as fur, that grows from the same place

Find out more

Books

Rainforest Animals (Focus on Habitats), Stephen Savage
　　(Wayland, 2006)

Usborne Beginners: Rainforest, Lucy Beckett-Bowman
　　(Usborne, 2008)

Websites

www.durrell.org/animals/mammals/redruffed-lemur
www.arkive.org/indri/indri-indri/

Index